Big Machines At Work

Snowplows

By Hal Rogers

The Child's World® Inc.

Published by The Child's World®, Inc.

Design and Production:
The Creative Spark, San Juan Capistrano, CA

Photos: © 1999 David M. Budd Photography

Library of Congress Cataloging-in-Publication Data

Rogers, Hal
        Snowplows / by Hal Rogers.
                p. cm.
        Summary: Describes the parts of a snowplow, how it works, and the work it does
to clear the roads of ice and snow.
        ISBN 1-56766-756-2 (lib. bdg. : alk. paper)
        1. Snowplows—Juvenile literature. [1. Snowplows.] I. Title.

TD868 .R64 2000
625.7'63--dc21
                                                                                00-023085

Contents

On the Job

On the job, a snowplow removes snow and ice from our roads. Winter weather can make driving very dangerous. A snowplow helps keep travelers safe.

This snowplow has a **blade** on the

front and another blade on the side.

The blades push snow off the road.

The front blade pushes the snow

to the side.

Now the side blade can push the

snow farther off the road.

Sometimes there is ice on the road. Some snowplows have a sand **spreader.** Sand is stored in a **bin** on top of the snowplow. The spreader sprinkles sand on the ice to make it less slippery.

Some snowplows carry a special liquid that can melt ice. The liquid is stored in a big **tank.** A **nozzle** squirts the liquid onto the road.

Sometimes many snowplows work together to get the job done quickly.

A snowplow has warning lights that flash. These lights help other drivers see the snowplow as it drives in snowy weather.

Climb Aboard!

Would you like to see where the driver sits?

A snowplow has a steering wheel and

controls that help the driver run it.

Up Close

The inside

1. The steering wheel

2. The controls

3. The driver's seat

The outside

1. The side blade

2. The bin

3. The front blade

4. The nozzles

5. The tank

6. The spreader

7. The warning lights

Glossary

bin (BIN)
A bin is a box on top of a snowplow. Sand is stored inside a snowplow's bin.

blade (BLAYD)
A blade is a sharp metal tool on the front and side of a snowplow. It pushes snow off the road.

controls (kun-TROLZ)
Controls are tools used to help make something work. A driver uses controls to make a snowplow work.

nozzle (NAHZ-el)
A nozzle is a tip attached to a tank or hose. A snowplow's nozzle sprays liquid on the road to melt ice.

spreader (SPREH-der)
A spreader is part of a snowplow. It spreads sand on roads to make them less slippery.

tank (TANGK)
A tank is a large container that holds liquids. A snowplow has a tank.